Then and Now

Communication

Vicki Yates

www.heinemann.co.uk/library
Visit our website to find out more information about Heinemann Library books.

To order:
 Phone 44 (0) 1865 888066
Send a fax to 44 (0) 1865 314091
 Visit the Heinemann Bookshop at www.heinemann.co.uk/library to browse our catalogue and order online.

First published in Great Britain by Heinemann Library, Halley Court, Jordan Hill, Oxford OX2 8EJ, part of Harcourt Education. Heinemann is a registered trademark of Harcourt Education Ltd.

Editorial: Charlotte Guillain and Vicki Yates
Design: Victoria Bevan, Joanna Hinton-Malivoire and Q2A solutions
Picture research: Ruth Blair and Q2A solutions
Production: Duncan Gilbert

Printed and bound in China by South China Printing Co. Ltd.

ISBN 978 0 431 191829
12 11 10 09 08
10 9 8 7 6 5 4 3 2 1

British Library Cataloguing in Publication Data
Yates, Vicki
Communication. - (Then and now)
302.2
A full catalogue record for this book is available from the British Library.

Acknowledgements
The publishers would like to thank the following for permission to reproduce photographs: AKG-Images pp. **6**, **23** (Erich Lessing); Alamy pp. **10** (Mary Evans Picture Library); Corbis pp. **13**, **14** (H. Armstrong Roberts); Denver Public Library, Western History Collection pp. **12**, **18**, **23**; Dino Fracchia photography p. **5** (Photographersdirect.com); Getty Images p. **11**, **15** (Photodisc), **17** (Brand X Pictures); Photodisc p. **23**; Photolibrary.com pp. **4** (Adamski-Peek Lori/Workbook, Inc), **8** (Nicholas Pavloff/Photonica Inc), **9** (Ramsey Patrick/ Imagestate Ltd/), **16** (Lebrecht Music And Arts Photo Library), **19** (David Grossman/Photo Researchers, Inc), **20** (Emilio Segre Visual Archives/Science Photo Library), **21** (Crittenden Guy/Workbook, Inc), **23** (Ramsey Patrick/ Imagestate Ltd); Shutterstock pp. **7** (Dubassy Photography), **22** (J. Helgason Photography).

Cover photographs reproduced with permission of Corbis: hieroglyphics (Bojan Brecelj) and keyboard (image100). Back cover photograph of radio reproduced with permission of Shutterstock (J. Helgason Photography)

Every effort has been made to contact copyright holders of any material reproduced in this book. Any omissions will be rectified in subsequent printings if notice is given to the publishers.

Contents

What is communication? 4

Reading and writing. 6

Telephones 12

Computers 16

Let's compare 20

What is it? 22

Picture glossary 23

Index 24

What is communication?

Communication is people talking to each other about things.

We can talk and share in
different ways.

Reading and writing

symbol

Long ago people wrote with pictures and symbols.

Today we write with symbols that
are letters.

Long ago people drew on cave walls.

Today we write on paper.

Long ago people told stories.

Today we read stories in books.

Telephones

Long ago some people sent smoke signals. The smoke sent a message to people far away.

Today we talk on the phone.

Computers

Long ago people wrote letters. They used pen and ink.

Today people write letters and emails.
We can use a computer to write.

Long ago people read newspapers.

Today people can read newspapers on the Internet.

Let's compare

Long ago there were fewer ways
to communicate.

Which is better? Then or now?

What is it?

This object was used for communication in the past. Do you know what it is?

Answer on p. 24

Picture glossary

Internet network of computers that people can use to communicate

message information sent from one person to another

smoke signal way of sending messages using smoke

symbol mark or sign that means something

Index

cave paintings 8

email 17

Internet 19

newspaper 18, 19

reading 11, 18, 19

Answer to question on p.22:   It is a radio. It was used a long time ago.

Note to Parents and Teachers

Before reading

Ensure that the children understand the word 'communication'. Ask the children how they could talk to their friends today from a long way away, for example using a phone, mobile phone, computer etc. Explain that long ago people did not have mobiles or computers so they had to use much slower ways of communicating.

After reading

• Make a timeline showing the ways people have communicated. Use a long strip of wallpaper and ask the children to draw different pictures to add to it: making smoke signals; drawing symbols; writing letters; listening to the radio; using the telephone; sending emails; using a mobile.

• Make a telephone. You will need two empty tins and 10 metres of thin string. Make a hole in the base of each tin. Thread the string though the holes and tie a knot.Stretch the string tightly. Ask one child to speak quietly into the tin and ask another child to listen.